How does one pray?

I have asked myself this question for years. I used to have a dedicated practice of being on my hands and knees before the Sun rose from her slumber, praying for our world, my family, neighbors, the community, and all I knew, near and far. Then one day, it occurred to me that life is a prayer. My feet are praying with every step I take. This compilation of poems is a living prayer to the wondrous world we live upon, with, and within.

May you find solace in knowing that we are together in those quiet moments of your healing, praying for the good of existence.

In service,
    Brigid

Love Letters to The Earth Vol 3

The Earth is my Prayer

Brigid Hopkins

ISBN: 979-8-9857324-4-3

Cover Design by: Nskvsky's

Formatting by: Michael Davie - grimhousepub.com/plans-pricing

Contents

Activator

The sacred activators
Like the trees, we all need a catalyst for our growth
Sometimes that may be fire to get our seeds to split
Sometimes that may be drought
Other times it might be plentiful rains
Never forget the sacred activator
It may come in the shape of a person
May come in the form of an element
It may come in idle conversation, but when you look
    back on the map of your life.
You will see the person, thing, or moment that
    touched you
In such a way that you could no longer remain in safety
    and sheathe of your skin
You slowly began to crack
I watched as that fissure formed a bigger and bigger gap
For your emergence

ANCESTORS

Beneath the ground
The bones of our ancestors

Carried on the winds.
Are the prayers of our ancestors

Poppin forth from the soil
Are the awakened roots of our ancestors

Now walking the Earth in the form
Modern man

No longer fighting for the equality of only one race
Now equality for the entire human race

Inviting Mother Earth to be our new battle of equality
For she is the most oppressed, disgraced, ill-treated of
    all her generosity

What began as inequality amongst humans has now
    evolved into a charity of our existence

In the grace of her dignity

ATTENTION

Love is trying to get your attention.
In a breeze
A song
A flower
Warm sun
Rustling leaves
A hummingbird
Unexpected phone call/text
Let the love that you are
Make its way inside of you.
Until you're so sure of the relationship
You gift it back out.

ATTUNE

Universe, please help me be the person I know I can be.
Please help me live from a conscious, consistent place
in my own heart, where I treat all of life with
respect, kindness, and understanding.
That I don't feed anger and rage when a mistake is
made, or I am feeling threatened or insecure.
Please help me to respond and not react or retaliate.
Please help me to be one who lives by her moral code.
Speaks authentically
Audibly
From my heart
Listening and honoring the many ways I can assist
each day.
Please attune me to be an instrument of peace and
kindness.
To color the world with more beauty.
To be a note in the symphony of life.
I wish to be a part of the song in harmony.
Please, Universe, I humbly request that you help me
get into alignment with this prayer.

AUTUMN

I could feel your approach
Before you rounded the bend
The desire for warmth
Conversations that stretch my ears
Fires
Nestled in the den
Of Autumn's
Hands

Crackling of acorns
Beneath my feet
Damp breaths
That only autumn
Hangs
I'm slowing
Turning inwardly
Won't you stay awhile
Tell me of your adventures
That blow you closer to me

It's been a whole season
My friend
Your embrace
Is most welcomed
Your hues invite

Brigid Hopkins

Me to relish my own
Spectrum and depths
Lay my head to reflect
On what is turning back
Into the soil
Of my life's experience

BELOVED

Thank you, Beloved
Thank you for the sun rays on my shoulder
The bird's chirps and tweets
The damp moss beneath my feet
I pray for abundance, and you give me this
With the numerous breathes in each minute
The beauty that befalls my eyes
And the relationships that encircle my life
I pray to stay present to the bounty and gifts you
    bestow
With your kind and gentle hand
Thank you for guiding me
Showing me the way when I am riddled with doubt or
    uncertainty
You pave a path that is just for me
Littered with the answers, I need
Thank you for the messages that come from you, my
    beloved
Through the face of another
I know it's you; it's often touched with a hint of your
    divine essence
Being passed through another's presence
Please help me to keep my heart open
To receive the love, support, and messages you
    transcribe

Brigid Hopkins

To help the healing in my life
I thank you for your friendship and loyalty
Please help me to keep my vessel clear
So that I may feel you near me for eternity

Bless Them

When passing an ambulance
A car accident
A firetruck
An animal struck by a car
A fallen tree
A homeless person asking for help
Anyone in distress

Instead of judging
Bless them

Offer a word of kindness
to what they are experiencing
They are you
We are they

BOUNDARY

Nobody shall cross my perimeters if they do not intend
good for me.

100 % benevolent good.

To be in harmony with divinity and God-sourced light.

I accept nothing less; I attract nothing less; I do not
allow anything less than 100% God source energy.

Real and true.
Eternally.
All timelines.
All gridlines.

So it is.

By the power of three x three

It's is declared
It is declared
It is declared

It is done

it is done
it is done

BUTTERFLY

Rapid growth cycles
Heavy breathing
Constant refocusing

Attending and Ascending
Setting intentions is only part of the equation.
The remainder is in orienting to said intention.
It is negotiating the tight corners and slivers of space to
    pass-through

Life is a series of decisions and consequences
To be fully alive, one must be ready to die
Turn to goo
Be limp and unavailable to the whims and mercy of
    another.

Only contending with what is most important as
    the time

Goo reorganizes, and it only happens through the deci-
    sion to live

I'm squeezing out of the chrysalis readying for the next
    cycle

CHEERS

Let us send our gratitude to all people whose purpose is
    to disrupt the systems.

The black sheep.
Non-Conformist.
The vocal.
The active.
The seers.

Your living is a sacred task, forging our evolution in its
    wake.

CRICKETS FALL SILENT

When all crickets fall silent
The wind stills
Dropping at my window
The immutable prayers
Of the Ancient ones
Mine
Yours
Ours
They breathed us into Now
Prayed a tomorrow
That we walk today

How I wonder
Is this evening so quiet
Are there no more
Praying for the future kin

The hopes of tomorrow's
Sinking in the silt of
Sorrows
Ego
Devilish pride
Where have all the prayers gone?

I lay my head upon the sill
My sensory sharpens
Only in the hum of darkness
Do I hear my unspoken prayers
Begin to coagulate
Rippling from my core
To be sung into the silent choir
Of nevermore
Their prayers did not fail
Nor run dry

The silence left room for humanity.
To be humbled
Return to grace
In this time and space
Letting our imagination
Be the doula
Of the future human race

Any frustration is like a setting sun whose view is
        obstructed
We are the visionaries
Birthed from the Ancestors
Who dreamed
Prayed
Progressed
The costs great
The history unbidden

We can move forward when
We let go of the remembrances
Become dreamers of what is good

Brigid Hopkins

In a kind way
For the next generation
Sitting upon a window sill
When all the crickets fall silent

DAWN REDWOOD

If you see me in public, you will probably see my butt
  first.
Most of my time outdoors is spent hunched over or
  bent over, taking macro shots of the hidden to the
  naked eye worlds and events just out of range.

This afternoon I was taking photos of the hardened sap
  on the base of a Dawn Redwood.
The sap looked like jewels strung along with the bark of
  her fulsome roots.

I heard a man say, "What is she doing?". A woman's
  voice said, "I don't know, but let's see." Soon, they
  were standing next to me. I stood up because it's
  not yet polite to meet people from behind!

The woman immediately got on her knees and started
  taking photos. She was astonished at how beautiful
  the sap was once she zoomed in. The man was less
  interested and went to their car.

She and I giggled, ooo'ing and ahhh'ing as we slowly
  circled the tree base of the well-decorated tree.
  Nature appreciation breeds connection, as glowing
  and solid as the sap running along with the bark.

DEAR ONE, AWAKEN

Dear One, Awaken
The alarm is buzzing
The children of today think we are insane
Why do we poison the people
The land
The air
The water
Why are we choosing to kill off the planet slowly
That has given us everything
What drives this insanity

One may say greed
Another may say industry
They may say money
Maybe one will have a hand on their heart
Whispering
Unconsciousness

They're not awake
They can't see
But You can
Waking one

Awakening doesn't mean the World is ready
To feel the deep sorrow that you face

The people may not realize their actions are toxic
They believe that the makers of these products are
    doing the right thing
They may not be ready to know they play a part too

Awakened one
I hear your pleas
I feel you are upset
I am with you

I, too wonder, and rile at the atrocities we are up
    against
The alarm is buzzing, and we have little time
Right these wrongs
Don't let that stop you
It takes a Carob tree seventy years to bear fruit
Plant them anyway

Every step you take is sacred
Walking atop your ancestors
Have you plunged your hands
Down
Deep within the ground

We walk upon sacred land
Tilled by the hand of your people
Mine too
The way they came to be
Is diminishing
We are evolving out of the colony
And Into sovereignty

Not to be confused with singularity

Brigid Hopkins

We have awakened
We are in this together
One people
One Earth

Your actions
Affect me
Mine affects you
We all affect faces we may never see
Species of all things near and far

Do not stop planting the seeds
Do not stop saying your prayers
Do not stop gathering in community
Keep lighting the way

There are times when I feel bone-weary
I just want to get up and run away
Telling myself, I have nothing to give
It's useless to show up

Earth never gets to say she's tired
Stops producing oxygen
Or she's no longer going to orbit
The Sun doesn't rise
She is tirelessly providing every minute of every day

The Earth gives us children
So we remember to honor innocence
Our temporary blindness to
What ills us is a forgetting
Of our nature
We are the Earth

Of her
From her
And will return to her

We live on borrowed time
But it gives us no right
To scorch
The hand that birthed us

Whenever I feel like I have nothing more to give
Or I'm exhausted

I can turn back to the Earth and see how she is limitless
In her ability to give
Anything that gets in the way of my ability to give
To Love
To be intimate
With the whole World

Is my forgetfulness that the
Clock is ticking

Listening from a disconnected
Sense of self
That never rose early enough
To sit and wait
As the Sun opened his eyes

Death and Love

I arrived for a lesson on grief and love.

I went down to the lake to process through some grief that's making itself known.

Grief from times I didn't take action.

Grief from trying to make someone else happy at cost.

Grief at seeing the tiny slivers of dignity that I gave away time and time again.

The grief of trading dignity like currency: for approval, validation, in one form or another, none of which mattered as much as I thought they would.

Even if it were a sincere offering from another person, I couldn't feel it because I was looking for my validation, my sense of approval.

As I continued along the shoreline, I felt a strong pull to go to the left, even though my mind said stay to the right.

I followed the pull and came upon this Cormorant. As I looked upon the carcass, I saw so much of myself reflected back to me.

I was facing the greatest fear, which was to die alone and forgotten.

I don't know if this is the same Cormorant that I've been watching for the last couple of weeks.

There was one with a gimpy wing.

But, if so, I wanted him to know that I appreciated him.

He made me laugh many times as I watched him get feisty with the seagulls.

I enjoyed his spirit.

My hunch is that based on how I felt and being called over to that area where this bird had passed away. It was the same one.

I knelt beside him, allowing the emptiness that I've carried, compounded with the fear that would never fill the vacancy, to move through me. I could hear many stories that I was defective in some way. Believing I had holes that reached through all time and space. I just kept feeling a deep sense of aloneness and forgotten.

I continued to sit with this bird. I thanked him for all the times that he flew free, enjoying his life.

Now he lay here returning to the Earth, I see him.

I see the parts that are missing in the full features.

I asked if I could offer anything to this moment, for the dying part inside of me that needed to be witnessed.

The shreds that are returning filling in my canvas. Returning to wholeness.

I walked and gathered Cottonwood leaves that I wanted to be a part of the ceremony. The Asters jumped up and asked to join the beautiful Cormorant with great glee.

I spoke blessings of love into a bird that I didn't know in the physical realm but reflected so many parts of myself that I didn't know. I didn't value them. I didn't pay attention. Instead, I kept looking at the faces around me, hoping they would see me in the desired way.

No one else can do that for me but me.

There are no mistakes that the eyes are missing from the Cormorant.

The eyes are a window to the soul, but not how we see through conditioning.

That sight comes from how we feel.

A few feet from me was this magnificent caterpillar. It was resting on top of the driftwood and making its way to green leaves to continue its journey.

As I sat with this being, I felt a sense of deep love arising from within. A love that is from me to me, moving freely through me. A love that reminds me of forgiveness repairs, and nature fills the holes.

DEFLATED

With emphasis on
Love
Light
Ascension
High Vibes
Tribes
And
Responsibility

After a big expansion
Comes the inevitable
Retraction

It can leave one feeling
A little
Less certainty
When deflated

It feels dense
Small
Isolating

Am I ok
To show up
When I feel this way

Brigid Hopkins

Will I detract high vibes
And ascent
When I feel like a
Shriveled balloon
Left to dry on cement

It's all a part of the process
No one more right than the other
They are cycles of growth
We all go through
When feeling and attentive
To the life moving through us

Be the puffy balloon
The shriveled balloon
The air in between

After all this life
Is one of many
Dreams

Departure

A little boy in a striped shirt is clinging to his mother's hand as she kneels beside him, scooping the cool river water into her free hand reaching towards his scraped arm. The sun is dancing along the surface, frogs are singing in the distance. The breeze moves around the two of them. Their life is my cinema.

I remember those days. Being with my littles. They're memories stowed within my heart. The door is slightly ajar, as I am in the middle of a transition from youth to early adulthood. Our eldest child has five more days of high school. He received his welcome packet from the University of his choosing, and the deposit has been paid for on-campus housing. I watch the young mother and child while also narrating my heart space to my dear friend who is walking beside me. As our time of change nears, I am breathing in between joy and grief, grief and joy. They share the same space ebbing and flowing throughout the day. I am pleased that our son is healthy and embarking on creating the life he sees for himself, AND I still reminisce over the days that belonged to us. There was nowhere to be, nothing to do, but enjoy the singing frogs and the breezes that stepped around us.

Brigid Hopkins

I remember strangers telling me to enjoy my time with
our children, for the minutes passed too quickly. I
would smile and nod, and uh-huh, uh-huh the kind
stranger that now resembles me more than I care to
admit. They, too, had a well of tears in their eyes;
the door to the memory chest must have cracked
open when seeing me with our young children.

Change is the cycle of life.

We are all moving along on some continuum. It takes
chance encounters to remind one of where they are
and what they have moved through. There is a red
Gerber daisy, slowly letting go of her petals, one by
one. She isn't fighting to remain in full bloom. She
has accepted that it is time to release the petals and
make room for the flower beside her to open.

Wherever our children end up in their lives, I won't
regret letting go and feeling the space that lives in
between each of the blooms. In the willingness to
release, my other hand opens to welcome what is
waiting to be greeted.

My heart is tender and awe at how life flows like a
river.

Dissolving Misdeeds

Great Wind

Please help me dissolve, transmute, transcend, remove,
and dispel, dis-create any curses, grudges, and
wrongdoing.

Any harmful thoughts, actions, words, intentions, and
deeds may be conscious or otherwise towards
another sentient being.

If I've held comparison, judgment, despair, resentment,
aggression, or anger towards myself or another
sentient being. Please help to remedy, repair, and
resolve this in all time and space, timelines, dimen-
sions, impressions, cells, DNA, forward and back,
through all generations, all ancestors, all the way to
the beginning, NOW.

Please help remove the effect and the imprint that my
unconscious or wounded actions, words, deeds,
thoughts, and intentions have created for any
sentient being.

Especially if said action, word, deed, intention were not
for their highest and greatest good.

Please help to remedy, repair, and resolve anything that
any sentient being or otherwise is carrying on
behalf of my unconscious deeds, actions, thoughts,
Ill will, or otherwise.

Please bring new health.

Brigid Hopkins

Please transmute
Please repair
Please elevate to the highest level of consciousness
available to us now.
Through all time and space
Please free anyone that has been oppressed, harmed,
suppressed, repressed, neglected, rejected, or
tormented by my thoughts, actions, words, or
deeds.
Please make this so, Now.
Thank you
Thank you
Thank you

DUALITY

I'm ancient and juvenile
I'm brave and a scaredy-cat
I'm passionate and lazy
I'm magic and practical
I'm a dreamer and logical
I'm confident and timid
I'm intriguing and an open book
I'm wise and ignorant
I'm creative and boring
I'm funny and laugh at my jokes
(Bcz no one finds them funny)
I'm adventurous and tedious
I'm spiritual, and I curse
I'm playful and serious
I'm gregarious and shy

It's not cut and dry.
These are examples of duality.
In between these states are many nuances that make
    me, me
Which is constantly evolving and broadening
I'm celebrating my duality more
Having less interest in flaws, as much as the spectrum
What may seem a defect, actually leads to my sublimity

EARTH TEACHERS

Today, I was sitting with this gentle being observing her preference for the sunnier patch in my garden. While still keeping a low profile in the foliage to keep herself protected and safe. It brought up reflections of what it takes to live life, to live a full life. A life of purposeful intent. A life where safety isn't as important as transformation.

This butterfly exists because she said YES to growth, the unknown. She didn't keep trying to fit into a box or image that didn't belong to her—dieting to be beautiful. Hide because of her shame of only being a butterfly. Change her appearance to be more pleasing to people. She didn't resist her natural process of dying, turning to soup, and transforming into her most radiant expression. She trusted her elemental cells to do what they knew how to do, morphing from a caterpillar, dying, being reborn as a butterfly. Death. Life. Flight.

Where in your life are you ready to say YES?

Travel
Relationship
Start your business

Try a new activity
Eat whole foods
Drink more water
Have the conversation
Hug strangers
Tell your story
Take up a hobby
Write your book
More time for play
New job
New house
Explore your creativity
Revisit your values

Are you tired of the same old story playing out in your
    life? You know the one. You've said it countless
    times and are exhausted. Tired of hearing it. Tired
    of speaking it. Tired of living it.

Can you surrender to the unknown and allow the meta-
    morphosis to begin? It starts with a YES.
What step are you willing to take to start your flight?

met·a·mor·pho·sis
noun
a change of the form or nature of a thing or person into a
    completely different one, by natural or supernatural
    means.

Economy of breath

When money is scarce, tied up, or lacking in some way.
I get to wondering.
What would it be like if I had to pay for each breath?
Every beat of my heart.
Each thought that occurs in my mind, yes, every single
    thought.
What would it be like if I had to pay my legs to move
    and my feet to hold my weight?
Would I ever worry again about buying food, clothing,
    accessories, travel, classes, a book, and lattes?
Nothing else would be possible without my breath.
True abundance is the wealth of this moment.
When we still have breath and choose to be grateful for
    that moving within us.
I'm very wealthy
I'm very blessed
I'm thankful for reminders that bring me into the
    present, where all is well.

EVERY DAY IS CEREMONY

Every day can be a ceremony.

Our heart the altar
Our intention is the theme
Our imagination the decorations
Our body carries the four directions
Our prayers are an offering
Our song is a thread that calls our ancestors, guides,
    and angels forth.

We are never too busy.
Too far away
Too alone
Too inexperienced

Ceremonies can be held singularly;
In a group
In-person
In cyberspace
In our daydreams

Let's give ourselves the chance to be in the ceremony.

Grape leaves

I'm curious about aging and what keeps one's vitality
going strong. This morning I was looking at our
grapevine. New leaves were unfurling in the rays of
the early dawn, quietly, unpretentiously, and
slowly opening their arms to embrace this new day,
their chance to bask in the sun's warmth.

As I looked further, the older leaves no longer had the
same luster as new ones. They are more velvety,
thicker, and consistent green. In contrast, the
younger leaves have a variety of hues.

I see these leaves as a symbolic way of understanding
integration. When something comes into our
consciousness, it's vibrant, bold, and fresh! We soak
it up, unsure where it will fit in, but we instinc-
tively know that it aligns with us. As we drink in
this awareness, we thicken our leaves and flush out
some of the brighter hues because they aren't yet
absorbing the sun's nutrients.

This transformation allows us to become fuller, steady,

and harmonious to our overall growth. The young leaves are tender, inexperienced, virgin.

My choice would be to nibble on the youngest leaves because they are most palatable fresh. If I were cooking with them, I would choose the older leaves because they're more substantial.

I think that vitality is the same way. We need new experiences to keep parts of our minds, body, and spirit alive with wonder and curiosity, yet to continue our journey's integration and steady growth are just as vital. I believe this is where the adage about balance is most applicable.

GRIEF

I am not sharing this because I need empathy.
I am sharing this because I have learned that grief isn't
    meant to be dealt with in isolation.
The weight alone can take us down.
I am extending my hand.
I am here.
You are not alone.

Grief hurts.

And...

The care, relationships, and love we share go beyond
    these pains.
I keep my hands and heart open because I can't hold
    it all.
It isn't mine to hold.
It isn't for any one of us to carry on our own.
The world itself is in a massive transition.
The sacrifices and loss are global.
They are not limited to one house, one neighborhood.
They are everywhere.

When we bump into someone that is a sharp edge,
Maybe they, too, are feeling the weight of grief.

Maybe they need a moment of grace.
Maybe they need to know they aren't alone.
Their sharp edge isn't a character flaw.
I am doing my best not to turn away from my edges and
    rough spots.

The time is right now
To accept
To be with
To make friends with the places that hurt.

When the air hits the wound, it heals.
It stings.
It hurts.
It heals.

I don't have any answers.
I don't know why.
I don't always have know-how.
I am putting one foot in front of the next.
I am showing up to life as best I can, with what I have
    in each moment. Some days are better than others.
A lot is being asked of each one of us right now.
Please know you are not alone.
I am here.
My hand is open.

GUIDANCE

Walking with a question, what is my medicine?
The wind invited me toward the North.
Cricket was there, first in song, then in conversation
Cricket says, "look at how strong I am even though I
   have a small body. My song carries far."

Then Eagle came and reminded me of my strength.
How far the Eagle will travel for survival. It doesn't get
   locked into one location or place.

Then I heard an entire course of crickets from all four
   directions.
They shared that my medicine is resonance, that reso-
nance is an undeniable truth.

As I was walking out of the forest, I picked up leaves.
As I was about to cross the bridge, a moth came and
   landed right on my hand.

I believe

I believe in God
An energy that is the creator of all things
Big and small
I do not believe in a big man in the sky
Holding a staff of judgment
Waiting to strike me down when I have sinned
I believe in mistakes
I believe in low moments
I believe that my God
Allows me to be Brigid
A human who came for an experience
Not judgment
To lead a life of winding missteps
Allowing me to fail
Fall
Climb
Each time I felt weary
My God was the fingertip on my heart
Reminding me, I am here
I am breathing
Try again
All of the shame
Guilt
Regret
I hold in my being

Brigid Hopkins

Isn't because I let my God down
I let myself down
The self that has held standards dictated by society
A society I do not align with
My God has always allowed me
To be sovereign
Not a drone
Letting my inner knowing lead me home
The same home my God lives in
The place I keep sacred
Expanding
Well insulated
Beginning with H
Beats
Ends with T

LIFE AS AN OYSTER

There is a precious balance between force and resis-
  tance, like shucking an oyster.
The oyster doesn't want to open prematurely,
  protecting itself from the invasiveness of the
  prying.

The shucker wants nothing more than to harvest what
  is inside the shell; will it be the pearl?

So the dance begins, and the force/resistance contin-
  ues, until....
The breathless moment both surrender at the exact
  moment. POP!

How often in life are we ready to take a leap of faith,
  and we repeatedly resist because we are unsure?

We don't know if we are the oyster or the shucker, but I
  believe we are both.

We fight the opening while simultaneously applying
  the force.

LOVE

When I look into your eyes
What I see
Are all the versions known to be
Once pain
Shame
Uncertainty
Fear
All brought you here
You've woven a peculiar path
Up and down
Under over
Never quitting
You believed that one day
The pain around your heart would fall away
It took more than hope
Giving breath to each new day
It was fire
Air
Water
Earth
Gave birth
Here you are
Warrior
Sovereign one

Dreamt into reality
Claim your destiny

Moon Tides

I continuously learn from the New Moon; whatever I
release during the Full Moon comes to be because I
unearthed it during the New Moon. The New
Moon often takes me into the abyss, the depths of
my deep familiar parts, that place I think is healed
or transformed, only to be shown another layer.
This deep dive is not an easy process but a neces-
sary step in moving into the place I know is
possible.

The place I am intending.
The place I am envisioning.
The place where I am an integrated soul.
One who walks with her light and her dark shadows
unapologetically.

I am making progress, and it is during the moon cycles I
find any place that is ready for my tending. Which
inevitably helps me to be more whole.

This cycle is showing me where I am empowered. And
where I still feel small, unsure, and scared.

I'm on a teeter-totter of growth. I go up and then back
down, up and down. What matters isn't the motion

but the awareness with each rise and resting place.
I am healing my perfectionist. The way I am doing
this is by paying attention. With my understanding,
I learn what has kept this behavior in place.

My perfectionist protects me

My perfectionist has high standards

My perfectionist has unrealistic expectations

My perfectionist can be a bully

My perfectionist keeps me striving for unobtainable
goals

My perfectionist isn't a realist

My perfectionist isolates me

My perfectionist delays progress

AND

My perfectionist is an underdeveloped part of my
psyche

My perfectionist has caused feelings of being
inadequate

My perfectionist learned that if she did everything
perfectly, there wasn't a "reason" for her to be
ignored or abandoned. Because she was perfect!

My perfectionist never learned to self-validate

My perfectionist wanted to be safe from criticisms -
they made her feel alone.

My perfectionist means well all the time - she needs
reminders that her best is GOOD ENOUGH.

My perfectionist is begging for someone to notice how
hard she tries -- this is my job.

My perfectionist is seeking love and acceptance -- I
adore her

It is a humbling experience to walk with your shadows
in the open. I have made numerous mistakes these

last few months while learning new skill sets and going after huge dreams and goals. I have fallen on my face. I have let people down. I have disappointed myself.

I KEEP GOING.
I acknowledge my part.
I apologize.
I learn.

I try not to repeat the same mistake, and when I do.
I take responsibility.
Responsibility is one aspect that my perfectionist tried to avoid for a lifetime. Something so simple that is excruciating.
Taking responsibility is acknowledging that I am not perfect.
It may seem simple or obvious, but it has taken me many growth steps, mentorships, and experiences to be where I am.

HUMBLED

I am not here to be perfect
I am here to learn
I am here to grow
I am here to integrate
I am here to expand
I am here to give
It doesn't have to be perfect
I am enough at any given moment
I can ask for help or to be witnessed
If I don't like how I showed up, I can correct my course

I have the power to be the woman I choose to be
It starts with being honest with myself
And liking the whole me
Not wishing away my shadows
To only be in my light
My shadows are a gift
My light is a gift

The moon, while unrelenting in her delivery, is also a
    gift.

I am wiser for receiving her medicine and being kinder
    to myself
There is a lot of healing work to be done for our world,
    and it begins here
The soft space in between my shoulder blades
Housing the goodness I was born with,
My heart.

New way to be Dramatic

Dear Universe,

Please help me soar free and high with a conscious
strategy that offers my whole authentic self to be
consumed by the world.

Please help me be steady as a fungus and bright as the
sunflower.

Please help me to hum like the bees pollinating our
tomorrow.

Please help me be a cloud that dances on the horizon,
reflecting the reach of the Sun.

OCTAVIA

I am walking my usual route in the grocery. I'm
    noticing my body and heart are not in sync. I feel
    heavy, weighed down with a hint of frazzled. I slow
    my walking speed to sync up with my breath. Time
    has shown me that hasty shopping results in poor
    choices and wasted food.

I want to be here.
I am here.
I keep walking.

I'm through most of the trip, entirely in my body as I
    make my way to the spices. I see a woman in a
    striking yellow dress as I round the bend. The color
    is bold and vibrant; it uniquely accentuates her
    shimmering brown skin. Her hair was wrapped in a
    sacred geometric shape. Her shoes are as bright as
    her dress. Everything about her is singing! She
    looks up at me, staring at her. I blush as I say, "I'm
    sorry for staring, but you are stunning. You are a
    beautiful woman."

Inside of myself, I immediately tap into that place
    again. The space of either I know this emotional
    state too well, or it's a new sensation that I don't

know well enough. My nerves feel on edge, and my stray strands of hair that don't quite make it into the ponytail reflect my inner state of being.

I tell her; I can't help but notice you remind me of the Sun. She laughs and says, "thank you." She proceeds to tell me that after the past few months she has had, she chooses to put on her finest attire every day and affirm that today will be ok. She wants to present that in her daily doings that she has touched a place of inner peace and knowing that she will always be ok. We introduce ourselves; her name is Octavia. She has recently laid to rest her best friend, her mother, and is recently divorced. She said, "by all accounts, I should be going crazy, but I am not. I feel at peace. There are just so many things we can't anticipate or control. But I can choose my peace, and I can choose my dress!

At this point, I am completely teary. I wonder to myself, how is it I have become so fortunate as to encounter her on this day, at this moment?

I say to Octavia, "I hear you, and thank you for being a messenger today. You have blessed me with your radiance." She said, "it's my pleasure, and I am glad we met. I hope to see you around; I am always here."

That last sentence struck me. At that moment, I had zero doubt that I was talking to an Angel. They are always here.

OFFERING

When each of our children was born, we wrapped
    them and took them to the woods. Laid them upon
    the forest floor and thanked the Creator for the gift
    of this precious being.

We promised to do our best to show them the way.

To care and nurture them with all we had.
We asked for help from the Creator to show us when
    we were lost or frightened.

As they've aged, I see that we stepped farther away
    from asking.

Put up a shield to protect our tender heart as each child
    ages.

The Creator didn't leave us or move far away.

But gave us time to flail, stress, worry, and struggle;
    each experience helped us find our way back to the
    one who birthed us.

Received with open arms and a welcoming of love
    unending.

Brigid Hopkins

I, too, was once laid upon the Earth and revered.

I, too, am a child of The Creator.

Never forgotten
Ignored
Disapproved of
Unwanted

But trusted
As love does
Love lets us wander
Love lets us try
Love allows us to take risks
Love watches patiently
As I work with guilt, shame, regrets.

The Creator knows my heart
The heart of each of their children

Always greeting us with love
It is our choice to receive or deny
Love is there
Patiently waiting
Always with care

Will you meet Love there

OPEN

If you have a savings account -- donate
If you have spare time -- volunteer
If you have a full fridge -- share
If you have peace -- share
If you have health -- volunteer
If you are lonely -- volunteer
If you pray -- pray for all
If you laugh -- laugh for all
If you can dream -- dream for all
If you care -- show it

Our world needs us to stand up and be givers. Any
    excess or abundance is an invitation to share with
    more than you're accustomed to.

Our world needs our dreams and vision of a better
    place.

Our world needs healing from greed and separation. It
    begins with one and ripples to all.

Our world needs our light to shine so brightly that
    darkness is a concept, not reality.

Brigid Hopkins

Our world needs your Goodwill.
Please give it
Please share it
Please Spread it

Be the Act of Goodwill in motion.

PLACES I GO

These places I go
Inside of my head
Leading me through
Corridors
Of blame
And worry
Hard to lift my head
I hide
Stay in bed
There is no place I want to tread
In this space
I'm most likely dreaming
Tied to machines
Traveling in space
An alien
To my hand
This land
This place
Where do I fit
Do I belong
It all is snug
Constrictive
Feels wrong
I'm longing for a place
I call home

Brigid Hopkins

Free to roam
In my delusion
No longer bound by convention
Invention
Rationale
It's all blowing up
Consumerism
Destructivism
Altruism
I lay
In my goo
Of blues
Wondering if they'll
Report about me on the news
Too soon forgotten
Too late to be known
Another angel went home

Pledge to Humanity

I pledge;
To say kind, uplifting words to myself & others.
Daily self-care, my cup must be filled.
To extend my hand, ears, & heart to others.
Not fixing their problems but supporting them as they
tend to them.
To listen with an open heart.
To say I'm sorry.
To say I don't know.
To sit with my triggers in place of hurting others.
To smile often, because it makes me happy.
To try new things.
To see beauty in everything.
To have the ultimate faith in my path.
Live in unity with my soul.

PUDDLES

Some people are similar to puddles.
They're lots of fun to splash and play with; they evaporate when the sun comes out.

Recovery

Four days in, I feel that my door opened to the Aunt
who has endless stories to tell, but there's no water
in the kettle, and the cupboards are bare. We sit
together cold and empty as the stories march along
my consciousness. Hard to follow along. My mind
is tired, distracted, hallow. A window where the
breezes blow and nothing sticks or makes any sense.

This visitor came in a flash, and we are learning how to
coexist inside my vessel. I heard the news and knew
that Omincron was in the air. Now I am living with
it inside of my body and home. At first, I wanted to
rally and push through the New Year. Like there is
a destination or somewhere to get to when the bell
strikes midnight.

Instead, I opened my hands and laid my head upon my
pillow. I put on my mask and asked my family not
to come into my room. I am now in quarantine.

Though my body aches, my head is pounding, and my
throat is cloggy. I know that my body is strong, and
everything will go as needed.

This visit isn't a test of endurance or some reminder to

blame me for not getting a booster shot. It's an invitation. A doorway...

Through which I have the chance to storm through, walk through, or stand at the precipice, I still have a choice here, with the virus in my body. I choose not to be at war or resist what is happening. I want to see the ways my body responds to the virus.

Here are a few things that I find fascinating about this experience.

The deep state of fatigue - I can look at this as Covid's fault, for *making me so tired*, or I can see that I am already THIS tired, and I now have the opportunity to rest.
The guidelines suggest that I do not leave my home or be around anyone else for a minimum of 5 - 10 days.

The fogginess and inability to think clearly - I can blame the virus or welcome the gibberish, nonsensical things floating around. I can spend more time looking out my window and meet the sparrow family that has taken residence in the bushes. One of the pair comes and sits at eye level. I look at Sparrow; Sparrow looks at me. We are communicating from a different level of language. The head nods are clear, and I feel the comforts of having a visitor, even if through the glass.

No taste or smell - Now, this was intriguing to me. I feel that this part of the infection has led to great enlightenment. I spent years reading books on mindfulness and tracking my thoughts, not being my thoughts, becoming the observer. I will say that I am good at seeing my thoughts. And yet, here I was, seeing something entirely new. I noticed that I kept thinking about frosted sugar cookies. It is the holiday season, so that makes sense that I have had a delicious cookie, and I am thinking about it. But, my body didn't want this cookie. I can't taste or smell anything. When I asked my body, "do you want a cookie." Immediately, the response was no. But my mind kept going. We must have this cookie; think of how good it will taste! How sweet and enticing the frosting is. My mind was trying to convince me that I would enjoy the cookie. It would be a doughy clump of tasteless sugar and flour bouncing around my mouth. I didn't want any food! How much of what I eat is driving by my head and not my instinctual need to replenish!

The waves of varied energy - One minute, I am ready to scrub my entire house; only two minutes later, I need to crawl back into bed. Anything that is a vertical experience needs to happen in my imagination because standing up for long periods is a direct invite to dizziness USA. The whole room spins, and I can barely make it back to bed.

Gratitude - I can't emphasize this one enough— everything we do in a day. From waking to bedtime has an impact. There are thousands of things that I do automatically that I have to negotiate and consider right now. Do I want to stand up to brush my teeth? I am wearing a mask; maybe no one will notice if I don't touch them. My hair is getting matted (curly hair problems), but it takes energy to brush my hair again. You get the picture. I am grateful for all of the means and measures available to keep myself clean, nourished, and hydrated. Trust me; you can find 1000 reasons to be thankful in the first few hours of your day!

Water - If I haven't thanked water enough. I will adequately thank the rivers and streams that lead to the pipes in my home that deliver fresh water every day. This life-giving fluid is the only thing that I routinely took in. My body knew I needed water. For which I am immensely grateful was available to me. Something I have taken for granted, I hold with more reverence and appreciation than ever before.

Breath - The scariest part of this virus is feeling like I am recovering, only to be completely blindsided by the lack of oxygen filling my blood. I was sitting, not standing or moving about, I noticed that I was breathing, but it felt like I wasn't getting any air. I remember this place because it used to happen when I would have panic attacks. I knew that panicking right now would NOT help my air intake or regulation. I had to keep telling myself that I was still breathing and that whatever was happening right now, I would be OK.

My son ran to the store to buy a pulse oximeter. During his trip to the store, I was walking deeper inside of me. To get into a calmer state and investigate what was happening.

I walked through this door of fear. A place I can't quite describe but was authentic at the moment. Fear welcomed me and sat my ass down. You see, your body has automatic processes. I am a virus interfering with this process, and you, the one watching me, are terrified of being out of control. You never were in control of this process. Your breath is operating all on its own. It isn't yours to control.

Right then, I fully relaxed and let everything sort itself out. When I thought I could control my breath, I added the stress and pressure into the equation. My body was handling the interruptions, but it also dealt with me, which was a double whammy to my system. Fear showed up to remind me that I controlled the anxiety, not my breathing. I kept inviting more trepidation because I wasn't trusting myself. My body or my breath to do what it needed to do. I called in more fear, not less, in the surge of anxiety. I was giving myself more of what I didn't want!

I gave up and handed myself over to the intelligence of my body and got out of the mind. This mind that lives at the top of my neck is an interesting character.

Day five is swiftly approaching, and I see the horizon of something different approaching. I do not know what tomorrow holds, but for now, I am aware of where I am and what I can do with the virus that has come to visit.

Brigid Hopkins

Stay hydrated
Rest
Talk to the birds
Keep a pulse oximeter and thermometer nearby
When in doubt, test it out. Take your temp and pulse.
    Make sure you are oxygenated.
Did I mention staying hydrated?
Do not eat too much or often
Keep your body warm and clean
Let yourself be a part of the experience, stay present

Give gratitude for everything you didn't notice you
    weren't grateful for before!

Remembering

Remember who we are
That's the message I keep hearing
To remember
To honor
To stay in step with remembering

Life has a way of rushing living
If we hurried our breath, we could faint.
Even if we don't fall over, does that mean we are not
   hurrying?

Watching the speedometer of our experiences is condi-
   tioning.

Do not step faster than our shadow
Walk with the Winds
Stay for the whole song
Our body
Our cells
Our souls
Our ancestors
All are reminding us to remember

Stay with our body
Stay on this breath

Brigid Hopkins

Stay in our light

Remember who we are
Why we are here
How we impact the tone of the crows call

Remember. Remember. Remember....

River of Sadness

As many in our world cry
Most feel the reverberation
And don't know why
Acts of aggression
Are repressed expression
Of deep sadness
Acknowledgment
That we are, in fact, connected

If we gave ourselves the chance
To feel the intricacies of
Life that connects
Rivers flowing around the world
Giving vitality
Refreshment
Purity

In the depths of sadness
There is love
In the ecstasies of rapture
There is love
In the madness beyond our control
There is love
It is the judgments we place that remove
All from the experience

Brigid Hopkins

Of what it is to live

The range of life
Are death and rebirth
Moment to moment
Each exhales a death
Each breath is a rebirth
All connecting back to the one
Who breathes through us

When tragedy strikes in the world, we can all feel it
Whether consciously or not
We are one heartbeat
One breath
All leading back to love

Ruts

The worn ruts
Come from a sense of comfort
Repetition
Endurance to live, is not living
The harder the waves crash upon your shores
The stronger the calling to soften
Open
Listen
Invite in possibility
Things are ever-changing
Impermanent
The illusion of grabbing
Digging
Or rutting in
Will not change the intensity
It will not protect one from
Inevitability
What is meant for you
Will come
Either as a gentle breeze
Or high tide
There is choice
There is control
It's not outside of you
Though

Brigid Hopkins

It's in your heart
Honoring
What is true for you
Not what you "should do."
Who you "should be"
What looks good to him, her, or me
Heave yourself out of the rut
Get comfortable with
Being uncomfortable
Let life see that you are no longer adversaries
But a team
One can never know how grand the view
When buried up to their neck in distorted sight
Give life your hand
Let it lead you
The end is the same for all of us
Choosing possibility
Pleasure
Mystery
That is a portal for those living above the rut

SILVER PLATTER

I am excited to step into the reality of *not hard*

We ask
We believe
We receive

I call this cycle the silver platter
This next season of life decadent

Ask and receive
Dream and manifest
Live and breathe with ease

I'm recycling the belief that attending any venue of life
    is hard; or what I most want to create is impossible;
    it's too big, too much, too grandiose.

We are a creation of God
Nothing is too much!

This is who and how we are
How we were created
To believe in these abilities changes the infrastructure
    of social norms

Sisterhood

She is my sight
When I am blind
The hand that reaches me
In my depths
The mother to my children
When I am nursing my wounds
Keyholder to my heart
In the tenderest times
Stoker to my flames
Encourager of my dreams
Laughter in the silence
She came when I called
But never picked up the phone
Hugged me when I was cold
But never shivered
Walked beside me on the winding path of uncertainty
Loving me as I am
Holding me in her being
She is my sister

Soothing Ways

Warm showers
Leaves dancing on the winds
Sounds of birds in the dawn
Ripples of water nearing a waterfall
The crispness of my breath in the cold air
Summer rains
Splashing in puddles
Laying on the grass
Sitting with the sunrise
Staring into the center of a flower
Watching the ripples on the water's surface
Sinking my toes into the grass
Watching clouds pass overhead
Taking long walks alone in nature
Cooling my feet along a stream
Standing with my arms outstretched in the winds
Feeling moss in between my fingers
Laying face down on the Earth
Listening to music
Drawing
Photography
Laughter
Meditation
Crying
Making tea

Brigid Hopkins

Harvesting dandelion greens
Ceremony to honor the moon cycles
Listening to others speak from their heart
Reading
Stirring golden milk
Making chai
Petting my dogs
Talking with my children
Car rides in the country
Walking around my yard
Calling a friend
Holding a stone
Cuddling
Caressing

SPRUCE OF DEVASTATION

On a regular day's commute, you captured my
    attention.
Maybe it was the lighting.
The glisten.
The red light.
Something in the ordinary stood out.

I noticed you.

Hello, I said. I will be back.

I finished the route and returned.

There you stood. As if time itself had no existence.
Irrelevant to your continuance

You are
And now, we are.

The knee-deep snow didn't deter me.
The frigid temperature drove me closer.

I stood in your majesty.
A solid community
Touching the heavens.

Brigid Hopkins

You rock and sway as one.
The sun, squeaking through and around your stature.

Try as I might, I can't capture the melody
You create in each caress of the wind.

I concede to witness and praise you.
With words and gaze.

In utter amazement
All my years of driving this route
It is today that you stood out.

The sun shifts.
My fingertips burn.
I know it's time to turn my attention
Towards warmth.

Two days later,
Tears replace the burn.

My heart agonizes at hearing
The turn of the saws blade.

The majesty of your community,
Now turned to tragedy.

You lay on the ground that was
The sound room floor to your melody.

How can this be?
Why?

I plead and gawk at the insensitivity
Of the hard hats tramping about.

Do they not see
Your royalty.

They should be on knee and bow
Not plow through your history.

Spruce and Pine
I may never know why we
Depend upon your wood
For our goods.

Please accept my apology.
The time we spent though brief
Is now a living Eulogy
In my Cosmology.

I will never forget
The way you sang to the heavens.

STORMS

The Earth doesn't apologize for her storms
Even when they create a catastrophe
That is a necessity for her proximity
The winds do not pardon themselves
When relocating an entire community
That is a necessity for their proximity
When did we learn to apologize
For the inner storms that arise
Why do we feel the need to hang our head
And walk sullenly

Storms
Chaos
Destruction
Are a natural part of reproduction
It's the ebb and flow
The give and the take

That is necessary for our proximity
We are a population of living things
Ever-growing and expanding

The cosmos
The Earth
You

Me
Every species

Why do we apologize for what naturally occurs
For the continuation of regeneration

The storms that are brewing in you
Become a part of the world
Whether intended or not
It's a natural part of the cycle
Breath
Energy

Let your storms be
Do not contain
Refrain
Or give apathy

Stop apologizing
For your nature
We need to purge and cleanse
Any sense of shame
That is a necessity for our proximity

Every one every second is evolving
Ascending
Stop devolving
Allow what is a necessity for your proximity

Responsibility
For the way, you carry your storm
Is to know it is the norm of experience
It doesn't have to be unleashed on another

Brigid Hopkins

Nor turned inwardly towards your shores

See it
Ride it
Feel it
Thank it

Storms pass
It's the aftermath we clean
What if
Cleaning could happen in the in-between

SUNRAYS

Please help me to be present and discerning of my
actions and choices.

Please clear away the fog of history to embrace the rays
of now.

Tiny Soul

I found the hornet laying in the walkway as if she were
     invisible.

I stopped and asked if I could move her.

It may seem "silly," but it didn't feel right to move her
     body without consent.

I asked to be shown where she would like to lay.

On our way there, I stopped and asked the clovers if
     they would like to be a part of her burial ceremony.

This event all happened during our son's football game.

I am thankful for the time to pay my respects to life, big
     and small
The deceased need caretaking as much as the living.

Every being is sacred.

TRAUMA ANXIETY

When you see a fidgety person, what do you think?
When you see someone standing off in the corner, what
    do you think?
What assumptions do you make when you haven't
    heard from a close friend in a long time?
If someone you know reveals that life is hard for them,
    what do you say?
If a friend is going in for testing of something suspicious
    on the ultrasound, how do you handle that?

There are so many life scenarios that catch us off guard.
    My immediate wish is to remove someone from
    their pain, lessen their worry, or swiftly lift them
    from their difficulty. I am not that powerful. Nor do
    I want to be that powerful. I most desire to connect
    with them and do it in a way that doesn't dampen
    the moment's intensity.

The intensity is for them; I am only the witness. No
    one is responsible for my discomfort or unease. The
    best thing I can do for the other person is sit in the
    fire with them and not try to fix or change anything.
To hold the space for their moment to be witnessed.

Brigid Hopkins

Even if I have never had their circumstance in my own
    life, I find a place close enough to have empathy:

I have pain
I have faced sorrow
I have lost
I have loved
I still grieve
I am healing
I have memories I wish I didn't remember
I have shame that still lingers

It is a gift when someone invites another into an
    emotionally intimate moment, exposing their pain
    and vulnerability. There is usually very little to be
    done and a lot of space between you. Any tensions
    or worries that unfold can be whisked away.

If you intend to love the person unconditionally. You
    can soothe yourself with the knowledge that you
    are enough.

That is why they invited you into their pain.

Transitions

My Mother, whose name was Faith
Taught me many things
The greatest of her lessons

Death

She was terrified to die.
But in those final days leading up to
The inevitable
Something changed

She began to see him, them; they
Her breath eased
Her body softened

Her story progressed from fear
To surrender
To knowing

All is going to be ok.

I never knew who he, them, or they were

Brigid Hopkins

I only knew at that moment after sitting in the room
    with death
As the invisible visitor

That we are never far from its sight
Death is here
Right his moment
Walking with each of us

It is our decision if we welcome it as a guest
Or
Deny its existence until the inevitable day arrives

Life and Death
Are as intricately coupled
As Joy and Grief
Inhale
Exhale

I breathe both

Turning Soil

I am feeling backward motion; it's as if I am cleaning
   one thread of a web of disappointments every day.
   The dreams I kept sewing and praying into now
   stagnated into the corners of my disbelief and
   dismay.

Why didn't these dreams materialize?

Why am I still uncertain of my direction, course, and
   actual work in the world?

Why do I keep clinging to that which can no longer
   grow?

Wait, I've been shown many lessons of these past three
   years that are helping me to turn the soil and hoe
   the ground. I am adding nutrients into the void.

I am beginning from nothing and building layer upon
   layer.
I was stripped bare.
I was left to gather my serenity and try again.

This process has been a continuum.
Leaving me at the threshold of now.

Brigid Hopkins

Not retrospect.
Not what if.
Simply now.

These dreams are worth the time and prayer, and
    effort.
I am not only praying for myself.
I am praying for all of humanity.

My prayers may be answered by the next generation or
    two with grace seven or eight. I can not stall or fall
    back down because it isn't materializing here
    and now.
My humanness forgets that the vision is often more
    significant than my primary resources.
This is why I pray.
I am not doing this work alone.
Or solely for my gain.
I am here as a catalyst for change in the world.
I am praying for billions.
I see into the future dreaming forward what is possible.

I may never see the outcome. I can trust it is NOT why
    I do my real work in the world.

My work is to hold the vision.
My work is to hold the frequency.
My work is to keep believing without any doubts.
My work is to keep praying.
My work is to keep being of service.
My work is obedience to the infinite.
My work is to keep singing.
My work is to keep building altars.

My work is to keep cleaning the Lake shores.
My work is to keep hugging the trees.
My work is to keep walking with the winds.
My work is to keep holding ceremonies.
My work is to keep talking with my ancestors.
My work is to keep my channels open and available for
what needs to come through me without question.

These pressures I place on myself are old constructs
that made me feel of value. I was justifying my exis-
tence and how I spend my time because I was given
money or praise in return.

The place I walk these days is quiet.

There are days like today I feel bewildered and ask,
why did you choose me?
Am I doing this right?
Are you sure I am the one that can best serve this
vision?

How will I explain myself when asked what I am
doing?
I look so irresponsible!
Do I need to see the miracles to keep moving forward
and show my people I am not wasting my time?

These are all thoughts and emotions I move through to
be in service. I am shedding the old stories to give
way to something, the thing that is right for my
essence to carry forward.

My soul work may not look like his or hers.

And I can see now; that is how it is supposed to be.

Being a servant to service is just like art.
A creation that is fluid motion--birthed from inspira-
    tion, experimentation, and effort, there isn't a right
    way to create art.

There is only your way. The finished piece is in itself
    the miracle. I am going back into the mystery for
    more raw materials to sew into my garden of inspi-
    ration and service. I may never see the fruits, and it
    won't stop me from planting the seeds.

UMBRELLA

Shoulder me from the harshness
Stand over me
Securely

While allowing me to
Be my guardian

We are a team
You the vantage
Of height
Wisdom
Timelessness

Me
New
Suckling
Wobbly

Learning to move
On this plane of
Existence

I need to touch you
In my wandering

Brigid Hopkins

Feel your guidance
Drip
Hover
Over me

Still able to scratch my knee
Bleeding from the surface
Is to exist

Our roles are precious
With purpose
Integral

I lookup
You down
To see the horizon
Don't blink

Vines

Vines climb it's what they do
They use anything to get to the warmth of you
Blessed Sun

The closer in proximity
And vigorously growing
To reproduce the unknowing
They need support
Ways to live

A vine on the ground hardens
The one on the trunk nurtured

Does the trunk know its role?
To support the vine that is climbing with only its
    growth in mind
Its survival

The vine is no different than the girl who sits three
    rows back
Scared to death to be left in the pack of the unworthy

Unseen

The ones who inch along the ground

Brigid Hopkins

Trying to keep a low profile
Their struggle is hidden, unfound
Except to anyone with a vantage
To see the broader scope

To be a climbing vine
Leaves little hope for independence
It's your birthright to plant your roots

Dig deep
Reach wide

Give thanks for all that you imbibe
There's no shame in not knowing
That your vine embowered
It leaves you falsely empowered

It's time to uncoil your grip
Allow yourself to slip
Wilt
Decay
To rejuvenate
At a later day

Into the tree, you were always meant to be

Spread your leaves
Reach high
Bend and bow
Proudly as now you know
Your destiny

WAKING ACTIVISM

As I allow the trickling in of Joy
A tide of grief is rising
I have to wrestle this feeling like a gigantic Alligator
To see into its eyes
The eyes of grief travel through millennia
No beginning or end
The timeless suffering
It is incredulous to sit with
How can this be century after century
Harm to another
For the varied skin color
Taking Lands
Lives
Dreams
All ashes in the sand of our shores
This sand can't be stored
The grief must be unleashed
Felt by the masses
Before we can begin to release our defenses
To every eye, we see
Taking responsibility
The only division is the one we believe
Differences aren't to be judged or assumed
There is no shame in the deed
The way one lives in a house or tree

Brigid Hopkins

On a boat in the deep sea
What difference does it make to me!
The space around my heart is cracking, peeling
Allowing the lies I've been told
Or sold to me
To feel above or better
Than someone else
All this fucking privilege
It disgusts me
When I can eat whatever I want
But she can't feed her children
Who am I do have more
Unwilling to do the labor of tough chores
That she must do
No choice
No decision
Only division
By our democracy
I don't have the solution
I do have a voice
An ambition
To leave this world better than I found it
If not by my work
Deeds
Or legacy
By the heart that beats
The breath I weave
I can choose to feel the grief
The misdeeds
Of my ancestors
My society
I can choose to be kind
To all I see

The way I treat myself
Anyone else
And believe the best
Despite what I see
For humanity's sake
Every living being deserves to be considered
Even if it's only my dream

WATERFALL

Floating along in this daydream, I am in awe of the
force by which waterfalls exist. As the water gently
flows ever so casually along the river. It is steadily
growing in momentum and strength as it nears the
edge of the fall.

With nowhere to turn, it's the only option to cascade
over the edge in complete surrender. The destina-
tion is unknown. All it can do at that moment is
allow itself to be carried.

The waterfall is a beautiful representation of Faith.

If I were a waterfall, I would most likely claw and
scratch, grasp onto the edge, scared that I would
crash against a rock and die. But if that would be
my fate, can I escape it by clinging? At what point
would I have to allow? Life is always leading us.
When I watch a waterfall, it is effortless elegance.

The power of the elements in their full glory, air, earth,
water, working in harmony, one isn't trying to do
out or compete with the other. They are working in
tandem for the same outcome to keep the water
flowing.

I do a disservice when I try to grapple with life's
   requests. I do not know the outcome, destination,
   and seldom the purpose.

If I am to live a life of Faith, is it not my duty to be
   obedient and surrender to the will of flow?

The flow that carries me in the current of life.

Ways I Hunger

I Hunger for things that
Surround me every day
My senses too narrow to take it all in

I hunger for stillness
A stillness that can't exist in modernistic society
A stillness so still that
Crickets can exhale

I hunger for darkness
Night dark of night
Dark night of the soul
Darkness that lives in caves
Underground darkness
Darkness so soft
My nervous system uncoils

I hunger for sweetness
Not of sugar
Candy
Long gazes of silence
With nature and her kin
To have my cheek touched
By a passing hummingbird

I hunger for language
Ancient
Lost
Dialect
That is purposeful
Clear

I hunger for air
So pure
That I lose my orientation
Of ground and sky

I hunger for a life without
Schedules
Goals
Deadlines
Minutes
Free to roam and be lost for an hour
Or until my last breath finishes

I hunger for understanding
So deep
And vast
Not one question is left to be asked

I hunger for playfulness
Innocence
Veneration
Cleverness
Inclusion of
All things great and small

Brigid Hopkins

I hunger to be warmed by fires
Awakened in brisk rivers
Flashed by thunder strikes
and
Jete' with the stars

WEARINESS

There are times when I feel bone-weary and tired.
Times I sit in a circle all day, meeting my limits,
    wanting to get up and run away.
Hearing a familiar inner dialogue stating I can't give
    presence any longer.
Or I have a long-standing commitment I don't feel like
    showing up for.

These times of weariness, they speak,
As an invitation to look beyond my limitation.

The Earth never gets to say she's not interested and
    stops producing oxygen.

Or she's not interested in participating, and The Sun
    doesn't rise.

Whenever I feel like I have nothing more to give, I'm
    too tired.

I can turn back to the Earth to see how she is limitless
    in her ability to give.

Anything that gets in the way of my ability to give, is a
    chance to look into my limitlessness.

Brigid Hopkins

Where divinity lives.

Wild Fire

Do I know what another feels?
Watching the forests burn
The animals perish
Many populations without water or food
My only perspective is my capacity to assimilate what
    it might be like

But I don't know

I haven't been a mountain lion in this life
I'm not a tree
I assume there is suffering because I would be uncom-
    fortable
And yet I trust that the divine plan is

Just
Loving
Kind

That many realities of evolution are happening that I
    can not yet conceive
As my consciousness grows
My trust evolves

I believe in mercy

Brigid Hopkins

I believe in divine intervention
I believe in a complex web of order
I believe everything is giving itself to the greater good.

It may not look pretty
It may not seem just
It may look horrific
But do I, a singular human, honestly know the whole
    story?

Is it possible that evolution is happening in the wake of
    destruction?
Is it possible that the sacrifices of many are for the
    species as a collective, not only humans?
Is it possible we are watching parts of our systems
    crumble to give compost to new births?

What does it all mean?
Stay curious to the mystery

Some may argue we are facing the end
Some may say it was all out doing
Some may say there's no hope
Others there is nothing to fear

We are near the end
And also the beginning

The beginning of being aware
The beginning of dying illusions
The beginning of building relationships with nature,
    one another, ourselves
The beginning of believing in oneness consciousness

The beginning of our evolution as conscious creators

Maybe we've done this before
Maybe we are an experiment
Perhaps we learned something old, in a new way
Maybe what is falling away is the weight of shame,
    greed, separation
Maybe we are all walking the planet home
Home to a new beginning

WINGS

Feeling the butterflies wings
Many of us have been doing personal development
    work probably since we opened our eyes.
As we keep moving through this growth process, I can't
    help but think about the symbolism of the butterfly
    hatching.

There's an entire process that takes place before she
    can take flight.

The wings have to fill, and the only way they can fill is
    if the butterfly is going squeeze through the
    chrysalis well enough that all of that blood gets
    pumping.

I feel like that's where we are right now as a society, in
    that deep squeeze, and we're being given the oppor-
    tunity to fill our wings with our nourishment.

Not the conditioning of our parents.
The conditioning of our communities.

What do we believe?
What do you feel in your bones is true for you?
Without justification.

Without argument.
Without defense.

It's what you know to be 100% true to you.

Hang upside down in the truth of you until your wings
    harden
and we can take flight.

WITCHES

I was meandering down moss-covered hills.
I round the bend
Beckoned by your spells
Aroma of mugwort
Moving waters in the distance

A secret coven
Gathering under the hemlock tree
Speaking into humanity
Invocations for change
Dancing under the full moon
We gather
We offer our hearts to move eternity
Bring forth the new dream for humanity
They have burned us
They have exiled us
They have scorned us
But the fears they felt from not participating couldn't
    keep us away.

THE EARTH IS MY PRAYER

Every step upon the sacred body of Earth

Is an exchange

We receive
We give

The Earth receives
The Earth gives

The Earth isn't here to compost everything we generate

She is a teacher
A model
A guide

On how we can be responsible
Stewards of life
Creation
Expression
Existence

When placing our hands upon Earth's body
Do so with great care

Brigid Hopkins

The soils carry our stories
Our sorrows
Our tomorrow

The time is now to be aware
Generous
and asking for consent

None of this is OURS
We do not own the land
Our hand
Nor Borders
or time

We are here to learn,
To give
To share
To support
And to be kind
guests upon
The breasts of our
Great Mother

About the Author

Artist, soul cartographer, dreamer and free spirit, Brigid Hopkins is a passionate student of Mother Earth and a creative visionary who loves to enrich her community and work to rejuvenate the health of our planet. As an avid apprentice of WindWork®, Reiki, shamanism, shadow work, ancestral healing, and peri/prenatal education, Brigid seeks to illuminate a path to wellbeing and help her readers pursue life-affirming health and purpose.

As the author of her debut poetry collection, Love Letters to the Earth, as well as the founder of Impermasculptures, a devotional Earth Art practice, Brigid is committed to sharing her message and inspiring her community to care for our planet and live in tandem with the natural world.

Brigid currently resides in the beautiful landscape of Northeast Ohio, the unseeded land of the Erie people, with her family. For more information, visit her website at Theclarity-path.com